Dynamo

Dynamo

Luke Samuel Yates

smith|doorstop

the poetry business

Published 2023
by The Poetry Business
Campo House,
54 Campo Lane,
Sheffield S1 2EG
www.poetrybusiness.co.uk

Designed & typeset by Utter.
Printed by Imprint Digital
Cover image: José Guadalupe Posada, 'Corrido del Caracol' ca. 1899,
The Metropolitan Museum of Art.

British Library Cataloguing-in-Publication Data.
A catalogue record for this book is available from the British Library.

Smith|Doorstop is a member of Inpress
www.inpressbooks.co.uk.
Distributed by NBN International, 1 Deltic Avenue,
Rooksley, Milton Keynes MK13 8LD.

The Poetry Business gratefully acknowledges the support
of Arts Council England.

Contents

3

For my family

1

Going somewhere

The engine gave out when we reached the top.
We were on a B road going over the moors.
Horses grazing on their shadows off West
and in the other direction turbines
gesturing like air traffic controllers.

You walked down the road for a signal.
Mum stayed in the passenger seat
with the door open, drinking tiny sips of water.
Flies kept landing on her hands and hair.
I wanted to brush them away but didn't want to startle her.

Some way off you found it and called me over.
A swarm the size of a Cantaloupe melon
clinging to the trunk of a hawthorn. A ball
of bees, chocolate and khaki, barely moving
but all pointing in the same direction.

A planet of traffic jams. Going somewhere
but also not going anywhere. We watched
as some left and others arrived,
ignoring us, figuring out
what to do next.

If only we could work together
to get out of this fix, you said
when we were back on the road,
back on the motorway, with all
the other people, in their cars.

Snorkelling

I was on the beach.
You were on the beach.
The sea was half on half off the beach.
You filled a bucket with the shells we found,
pressed yourself to the ear of each in turn
and they heard your city, impatient and ceaseless
and you walking through it in your sunglasses and baseball cap,
snorkelling through the shopping malls,
the department store china set displays
and mannequin models listing in their underwear,
the crowds swirling around you in unrepeatable patterns
of desire, more complex than a Vitamin B complex,
more complex than a military-industrial complex,
more complex than *Complex*, the magazine for men:
Music, Girls, Style, Entertainment, Sneakers, Technology.

And you put out your arms in front of you but do not touch anybody,
and nobody touches you, they were always already leaving
a space around you, a space of you plus the extra they call personal space
around the bit that they call your place in society.

We're getting in the car as the rain starts to fall.
We'll keep the shells in a bucket outside the back door.

They were building something

They were building something
but first they were knocking something down.
They smashed the windows
with sledgehammers, wearing goggles.
Then they went in with a couple
of high reach excavators.

They took it away in pieces
then brought new stuff in on trucks.
Big grey girders, great sheets of glass.
Everyone I knew was drinking too much.
All I had in the fridge were lemons
shrinking and hardening.

They'd put some CG renders
of what they intended
on the hoardings around the outside.
Part of the building was still standing:
a door going nowhere, a staircase,
a phone receiver dangling.

Yet before long, people
with briefcases and coffees
would mill purposefully
around revolving doors.
They didn't look much like us,
or that they'd like us much.

The third way

He came over and we weighed ourselves.
He had the hiccups.
It was somebody's birthday
but we couldn't get to their house.

The river was brown
and the forest smelled of garlic,
the ground was wet, our trainers soaked.
There was pornography in the grass.

He told me about someone he got with,
wearing fancy dress. They met up the next week,
him on his bike, her in a convertible. She asked him,
following a long silence, 'So do you like films?'

We were getting towards the road
and the roundabout which had only one other exit
back onto the same road, over the underpass
which led from nowhere to a field.

I often feel that I'm coming up
to that roundabout. I've got choices.
I can come off onto the same road
or keep going round.

The pair of scissors that could cut anything

cut nothing at first. We had read the instructions
and kept them in a special box
away from everything
we valued.

But the scissors could cut anything
and they worked their way out after a while.
We saw them suddenly in the kitchen one day,
standing up on their shears
like a Gap model
before they disappeared through the floor.

We watched them on television that night
striding around the town centre. The police lined the streets,
guarding the property
in their serious costumes.

Birmingham New Street has ten different exits

and all of them go to Birmingham.
I give a quid to a man who asks
but there are more
than I can afford of them.

I eat my sandwich in a bus stop
on an angled metal strip
as a pigeon limps by on a stub of a leg
and pecks at something it has imagined.

There's a corrugated iron warehouse
with 'Goods Inward' on one side
and 'Aquariums. Greenhouses.
Packaging' on the other.

Perhaps, the warehouse implied,
our feelings about the West Midlands
should come from within. Caring,
cultivating, protecting.

And my dad's from Birmingham,
with his jumpers that smell exactly right,
his gentle voice. This place
is in my blood, and goods inward.

Suddenly I feel good inward.
The sun warms my legs
like a bull terrier's
breath. Here

is a functioning city with some economic
activity, culture, packaging.
The guy I gave a pound to has probably
already turned his life around.

On the corner, a small caravan
sells ice cream to teenagers
and a man in a claret and blue tracksuit
with a Selfridges bag he was given

gazes up at the sound
a seagull is making
as it glides above us,
thermal air currents

of modest hope and mild disappointments:
'Birmingham',
it calls. 'Birmingham,
Birmingham, Birmingham'.

The mystery shopper

The customers are like the universe, they never end
and one of them is the mystery shopper
for whom you must go the extra mile.

Some days when it's quiet
you work the trolleys
with Kevin and Mikey.

Kevin tells you about a friend
who broke his penis
through inaccurate sex.

Mikey tells us that when using the walkie-talkie
we should say 'Roger Roger'
before and after.

All this is banter.

But mainly you are just a conveyor belt
for thinking about
endings.

The most regular customer
is a big quiet man
who bought profiteroles.

To get the job they said talk about a time
you overcame a problem.
There was a team exercise

where you had to design
a new clothing line using bin bags,
sellotape, and your initiative.

Stopping the White Man March

The last time I was in Blackpool
we went to a demonstration
against something called the White Man March.

We took a coach from outside a park
and went to the wrong pub
on the sea front.

Then, kettled next to some flood defences,
we watched a police van
reverse into a bollard.

We managed to get chips
and although we mainly just stood around in the wind
we stopped the march.

It was at least as good
as any other time
I've been to Blackpool.

I remember the White Men
in front of a souvenir shop,
their arms outstretched

as though releasing birds
in a romantic
music video.

And one, forced back
by the police line, falling
into a stand of fridge magnets.

Hotpot

Tom is tidal.
He had too much broth.
The hotpot came with free top-ups
and Tom finished it off.

He can't drive his car
because of the moon.
He can tell the time
without a clock.

He's swallowing the sea,
he couldn't be stopped.
Maybe we didn't try hard enough.
Now the mountains are dessert

and yet everything else
carries on going.
The world
diminishes.

I cycle home
past the cranes
like horses sleeping on their feet,
the park moistening its lips.

The lights change on an empty crossing.

The bikers

The bikers climb the path we're coming down,
here they come now, from the beach
where there might be seals, should we
ask them if they've seen any seals?
We're asking them if they've seen the seals.
One has a T-shirt with the Iron Cross on it but we know
that doesn't necessarily mean they are fascists.

They have seen the seals, yes, there are many
seals, they smile, recounting the seals.
We'd seen their bikes at the top, a swastika
on one helmet, a little Union Jack shield,
and an I Heart EU on a fuel tank.
They love the EU. They love seals.
Iron Cross. We thank the bikers,

keep walking down.
It really is such a beautiful day.
We even see a deer at the edge
of the golf course, just a young one,
a Hitler youth deer leaping away through the gorse
and then cliffs come into view like a line
of bad teeth. And it's true, there are seals

lying all over the beach
curling this way or that
like opening or closing parentheses.
Others swim around near the shore.
The rain starts quite suddenly.
A man with his son searching for fossils
smashes up rocks with a hammer.

Signs

A bumblebee peruses the yard
like someone wandering into a bar
pretending to be on the phone
in order to use the toilet.

It's April and things are opening.
The roofers throw pieces of roof
off the roof. I get a delivery:
it's the clay.

I lie in bed in the morning till my thoughts
start straightening themselves out
like replacing a solid door
with a door made of glass.

We hire a van called a Peugeot Partner
and move you in over a weekend
and two packets of those chocolate biscuits
with pictures moulded into the chocolate.

The pictures on these biscuits
resemble tarot cards.
We must be attentive to such signs,
you tell me, putting one in your mouth.

We're unpacking boxes,
then each other.
This one is for the bedroom, you say,
leading me up the stairs.

Matinee

She looks good running
with an umbrella
and a ponytail
in the mist
to catch the bus
to watch the matinee
the day after she's watered the allotment:

the suspicious beginnings of gourds
the base of the bean toblerone
the rainbow chard
the brassicas in their enclosure
the compost where the ants live
when they're not in the artichokes

and from the old bit of carpet
where she covers the tools
to the raised bed
where she has poppies
stocks
and love in the mist
a mouse:

She looks good running

That I am so angry

I hate her hat. I say
'The people who wear these hats
are the same kind of people
who describe themselves as
high-powered'.
She wears the hat whenever she wants.

I say 'I can't stand him. He always interrupts me,
then when I'm not talking,
he apologises for interrupting me'.
She has also noticed that he uses the words
'connote' and 'academe'
but she thinks it is strange that I am so angry.

She keeps wearing the hat.
One day we go into town
and get cheese
and squid
and eat it with Polish bread
next to the fountain. She sits there

coolly eating a tentacle.
The children play in the fountain
and the wind picks up.

Finding Bobby

Bobby had a problem eating vegetables and fruit.
She hadn't had any since she was twelve.
Her bowel age was 71.
She put a grape in her mouth
but it just fell out again.
She started to retch.
She said 'It's as though somebody asked you to pick up
dog shit and eat it: you'd find it hard, wouldn't you?'

But she didn't look
at all malnourished.
The nutritionist said to her
'Your food is all the same colour isn't it?
You basically eat baby food, don't you?'
She said 'Yeah, I do'. The nutritionist said
'You eat like a baby, don't you, basically?'
She said 'Yeah, definitely, I do'.

She tried to eat a mushroom
but had to spit it into the sink.
The nutritionist was not very understanding.
She didn't understand Bobby, but I did.
I turned off the television, wondered
how I might find Bobby. What I would cook for her.
She already had a boyfriend and a child
but they all seemed easy-going.

'Broccoli is my Everest', she said,
laughing, ashamed.

Dynamo

On the way back from the shops
where I had purchased some essentials and a luxury,
I saw a line of seals loafing on the beach,
the sea crashing and foaming and the seals
unconcerned, shifting slightly in the waves,
crumbs on a talking man's lip.

My phone rang, it was Martha telling me to put the oven on
when I got home so we could have potatoes, which to me didn't
make sense because we have a fan-assisted oven,
but I said yes, that I loved her, she said she loved me,
I said goodbye, she said goodbye, that she loved me, I loved her,
I said goodbye, bye bye bye byebyebye.

At the garden gate a couple of bikes were locked on either side.
Their lights were on, they were dynamo lights
that were working off the movement of the earth in space,
like me, I thought, picking up the post
which was just junk mail
from broadband and satellite TV providers.

I got back and turned on the oven,
looked at the clock, adjusted my expectations,
opened the window and looked out. Across
the yard, in one of the houses opposite,
a woman sat in the window, talking
to another person out of sight.

The round blue box
that was always there on the window sill
was now in front of her, between them,
like a Ouija board, or more likely
a tin of children over which
they were busily establishing ownership.

2

Untitled 9-5

We did a reading in an art gallery.
We could hear a hair-drier in an installation coming on and off,
and the sound of either somebody walking in heels
or the knuckles of a labourer in a painted field.

The sun lit everything up outside the window like a stage:
a tall man making a sound recording of a tree,
two students in turquoise and ponytails
describing figures of eight around the park paths

and my life partner, or someone who looked
enough like her, overtaking them on her bike,
very upright in her helmet, the casing for a rare
and nutritious nut that I would never finish eating.

An artist had taken off her clothes
and was falling down the stairwell in slow-motion.
People came to see us, buy our books and look at the artist.
She would reach the bottom of the steps at closing time.

Mike and Annette's working week

That morning there was a hare
next to the swimming pool
in front of Mike and Annette's mansion.
I carried the thought of it about all day
till evening, when I left it where I'd found it
for tomorrow, hoping it would be a warm night
and that if there were to be rain
that it would be light and refreshing.

The following day there
was nothing to be seen of the hare.
Just the swimming pool
and behind, Mike and Annette's mansion.
An old cellist lumping his cello home
and a long van on the corner.

The next day the swimming pool had gone too
and it had become autumn,
the wind conducting leaves
off trees in sixes, sevens, flurries.
There stood Mike and Annette's mansion
looking very big and very white, and very big.

The day after was, the office agreed, a day to celebrate
but I felt guilty about what I had said to my partner
the night before, in the garden, bringing in the washing.
Walking home, I forgot to check for the cellist or the hare.

On the final day it was just Mike and Annette
at the end of the road in their dressing gowns,
with their kitchen appliances.

Annette was looking really tanned.
Mike was eating an egg.

The Flemish Primitives

The baby held a green parrot
as if to say *Welcome*
and the knight's breastplate
held a message for the saint
who he had been looking forward to meeting.
The parrot itself said nothing
but readjusted its footing
like a child experimenting with its feet,
and the baby stroked its green feathers
listlessly. In the distance stood a machine
with a great wheel turning at one side
and a giant cloth hanging over much of its workings.
They were building new countries in there
and the covered parts were taboos.
The saint thanked the knight,
accepted the parrot, took its head
with his other hand and twisted
as though the parrot was a drink.
But the saint did not drink.
He stood there for a long time,
the sun rising and falling behind him,
his face darkening and lighting up again,
clouding, clearing, shining.

Treading on another tall man's long foot
after Michael Donaghy

I am minded of the brother I never had:
a man who drinks mild
and has looked the same
since he was a child,

a fascinator
of posh women,
a top podiatrist, understated
prog rock musician.

We meet in town every few months
for a bad panini. He's on his way
to a conference on foot and ankle
research and treatment history.

In July we camp in the Peaks
with our kids and wives
and the large tents you buy
when you're settled in your lives.

We stand looking at the reservoir
from the bridge,
a couple of birds diving
into their own image.

On the other side of the lake
a third brother watches us
with binoculars, a couple
of red setters

and a bag of cooking apples.

Mars, surrounded by Arts and Sciences, conquers Ignorance
after Antoon Claeissens

It was a Tuesday evening
and there was nothing on worth watching.
Arts and Sciences had come over
and were standing around
absent-mindedly spinning orbs,
twirling their palettes, playing wind instruments,
mapping the known world.

Mars felt good when Arts and Sciences were around,
and Arts and Sciences could get on with things.
Today Mars felt good enough to take down Ignorance
in a judo throw taught to him by Jupiter, taking
one's opponent by the shoulders, stepping forward
and tripping them over your leg.
Ignorance lay on the ground, cursing.

Mars stood there with his foot
on Ignorance's throat for a while.
Arts played a catchy song
and Sciences did something clever
with a pair of compasses. When Mars
got bored he tried to kick Ignorance away,
but Ignorance was surprisingly heavy.

He just carried on lying there
wringing his hands,
distracting everybody
with his moaning, his paper cup.

Getting to travel a lot with your job

The swimming pool at the top of the hotel
is inert.
The water as still
as a dessert.

If I was with you
we'd go in.
I would dive like a spoon
then join you in the steam room.

You look out over the town.
Steep-pitched roofs covered in snow.
Napkins in a café
that you don't know.

You return on Sunday.
I feel like you're wearing
or doing something new.
I find you

in the big glass atrium,
kiss you between the bit
where they check your ticket
and where they sell you a baguette,

the edge of your eye.
I lump your bag into the car
and you get in
and we both sit there

in the dark
for the moment
before I find the ignition.
Take me home

you say in a voice
tired as much
of coming back
as being away.

Persimmon

We took the train
into the mountains
knees under sheets
printed with agricultural motifs

rented a barn
and picked fruit for cash
If people ate more fruit she asks
would they feel less alienated?

I already feel better just being around fruit
just talking about fruit
dearest miniola
my cherimoya

as we share a portion of chips on a wall
the evening settling
like a dog in a dusty room
her hand in mine not really moving

the cars lighting up
sections of trees
lining the B road
on the other side of the valley

people looking for a way
into the next part of their lives.

France

Suddenly, we were no longer in the tunnel
and had arrived in France.
French trees, French pylons,
French cows and French fields
stretched out ahead of us like a brochure.
The pylons held the cables under their arms
as they might baguettes
and the cows in the fields queuing
on their way to Camembert cheese
looked exactly like a string of onions.

Out there, in the centres-villes,
French ladies sat, smoking on stools,
their hosiery crossed and manners plaited,
kissing each word goodbye as it leaves their mouths.

In the buffet car a man and a woman were talking
about commuting in their shared second language.
The train tracks curved and they staggered
slightly forwards and backwards again,
as though demonstrating basic dance steps
and we passed a field of wind turbines, their great propellers
stirring the air into meringues
that only they could see
but that everyone could eat.

Can't

When she goes into that silence
he feels like the can opener
that rides around the edge of the can
without opening it in any way.
She could be a can of cool coconut milk.
She could be a can of plum tomatoes.
He is meant to be making a curry.
Settled and progressing in his career.
She is a can of implacable butter beans.
All kinds of possibilities
are slipping away.

After work

Late afternoon in June is the best time to run
for understanding the architecture of a city,
when the roads are clear of contradictions,
things blurring in the distance

because they are far:
a landscape gardener or a police van,
a skip with a pram or a zimmer frame,
a line of trees or a histogram

and the sound of a bouncing ball
bouncing around the terraces.

We spend the day with one machine
then go home to another.
I don't have the solution.
Just recommendations: books, films,

love, struggle, sleep.
We leave streams of pixels
on the pavements behind us, fallen
Christmas decorations.

After the rain the snow started

like precipitation
was a competitive sport.
The snowflakes got bigger and bigger.

We lined up snowballs on a car bonnet
but couldn't find the right person to throw them at.
The neighbour threw one at her dog.

On Clarendon Road, a man
was pulling his wife along in a sledge
and Sarah was in her window

gazing out like a cat
while The Godfather III
took care of itself behind her.

In the park, somebody was pushing
a gigantic snowball around. She stopped
to stretch her back, then got back to it.

The sky was nicotine.
We made snowmen
in our own image.

Someone said *Are you wearing
your jacket the wrong way round?*
No, I said, *it's supposed to look like this.*

The man on the plane had paid

The man on the plane had paid
for his seat and for half of each arm-rest
and for the space under the seat in front of him
and for one smile from this air hostess
and one goodbye from that air hostess
and two or three of the captain's words
and a few dozen miles of the journey
and a miniature motorway and village
and a lifejacket and a torch and a whistle and a tube
in which to blow, and an oxygen mask
and oxygen masks for his children
and for the probability that the flight
would reach its destination without incident
and a chance, if the plane were to unexpectedly land
and the cabin to settle intact in a forest or an ocean
to lift himself out and feel a few hundred drops of rain
fall and spread as though counting themselves upon him.

It wasn't the varroa

I kept bees in the noughties.
I had an apiary with a guy called Pele.
I haven't seen Pele now for a few years.
We fell out over something bee-related.

Colony collapse, they called it
in the United States of America.
After six years most of our bees had gone.
It wasn't the varroa: we were on top of the varroa.

Pele got into recruitment consultancy
and made considerable sums of money.
I told him I thought all suits looked the same.
I remembered he had always belittled me.

It's been a few years now since I've seen Pele.
I don't exactly have a job at the moment.
I buy and sell things on the internet. There are websites
where you can fill in questionnaires for money.

On the experience of accidentally preparing a vegetarian shepherd's pie in a bike basket on the way home

The lentil bag exploded as I rolled off the kerb. I passed the flats on the new estate, some men stood laughing on a balcony in trousers that did not reach their shoes. When I hit the first sleeping policeman the vegetables began to break into rustic bite-sized pieces. The rain was getting heavier. I went past the scrapyard, an unmanned crane was holding up a Nissan Micra as though it had been examining it before falling asleep. The month was May and the climate was changing so it was not surprising that even before the last drops of rain had landed on my waterproof equipment and face, the sun emerged and began its routine. By the time I turned onto my road the vegetables had mingled, the lentils swollen, and a layer of mashed potato and grated cheese had spread itself over the top. It was baking hot.

The good morning

The room had the print of an iron melted into its carpet
as though the iron had tried to leave. There was
a broad canvas the dimensions of a television,
but the real television was mounted on a bracket
so that it could point at the bed, the chair or the ensuite.
The canvas was a mix of purples and greens
and in the foreground a couple of lavender spires
rose up into the painter's focus, a late
summer the room could only imagine
in soft focus and vague colours
due to its sealed windows feature
and the air conditioning system
that you did not need to switch off
and could not. Everything was in plastic
wrapping: the milk, the tea, the bed,
the television, the iron. The light
that came through the window was from
a large atrium in the middle of the hotel
which was itself only one unit in a larger
concourse of entertainment outlets
with an overarching ceiling. We made
a cup of tea, peeled the ribbon off the bed
and we lay down on it, slightly apart. The bed
was actually two smaller beds pressed together;
a king-sized sheet stretched tightly over the top.

3

Moving

When we stop talking
and you start to fill up
with the heavy dark chemical of sleep

I feel the inevitability of everything
and the occasional twitches
of your body resisting.

They might come from a foot
or a toe. They might come
from your arm stretched out

as though to break your fall.
And although I love
these tiny vibrations

like a boat rubbing
on something it is moored to
or must pass

to progress –
I can't sleep
living all this with you.

I move away so slow
you don't know
I'm going.

And the year you moved in

we lay on the couch
like Spanish question marks,
the things we'd promised
in the gaps between us

watching images move across a screen
and the people saying things in one language
and the words below in another
and then the meanings.

We thought things would change
when they made you permanent.
I was growing sunflowers on the wall
that backed onto the allotments.

The sunflowers grew like a bar chart
presenting possible answers
to a question
I had not asked.

Because that was the year
we transplanted the fuchsia
and it died but I kept
watering it anyway.

And then it was New Year.
We lit the chiminea
and sat outside, drinking
in our ski gear.

They're quite famous, apparently,

although *I* haven't heard of them.
Well that's irrelevant, she says,
which I suppose is true. She's
annoyed about something.

I spend my life working out what.
I drive to the office in my Peugeot in the rain,
in the sun. I eat from a tupperware
looking at my inbox.

Suddenly, she's moving out
and I'm getting into swimming.
Up and down the pool I go, plunging my head
again and again into the water.

The frisbee

The frisbee flies
like a moon orbiting the weekend
a fruit propelled
by its own sweetness

It leaves and it arrives
It is the line we write and rewrite
It is shaving the earth's face
It is unspooling hope

Its tiny wobbles
the warps on a record

It is a platelet hurtling
through a capillary
It is a soufflé rising and rising
It is a commodity

We think it will never land

Done up by the landlord

The pineapple plant displays its pineapple
like a trophy it has won
for having grown a pineapple.

It suspends it meaningfully as a man
holds a ball he is about to throw for a dog
that is so enthusiastic about the ball

it has forgotten what it is
and everything else if it ever
knew anything at all. She says

Did you know pineapples were once so celebrated
that your servant would wheel one out
to display at colonial-era dinner parties?

Now they are 99p in Lidl
and your mum can buy you one
in plant format.

We have a cup of tea. Her new place is nice,
it's only just been done up by the landlord
but he might have cut some corners.

Damp green shapes form on the floor.
She vacuums the green off
but it comes back.

I drive home in a ball of thought.
She's over there now,
and now I'm over here.

I run in the park and look up at the trees.
I feel my heart pushing the blood around.
Suddenly two years have passed.

How have you been?
I ask her. *Oh,*
you know, she says.

Forton, 5AM

The toilets are very bright and very empty.
It's just forty urinals, six full length mirrors
and a machine for selling condoms
or chewable toothbrushes.
I'll probably never buy
a chewable toothbrush
but I've thought a lot
about how it must feel.

Back in the concourse area the shops are shut
and they are putting tables on top of tables.
There's no couples with kids or kids
with pick and mix. There's no stag do.
The jelly babies in the pick and mix lie on top
of each other, faceless and without futures.
The snakes in the pick and mix are soft translucent
reptiles made out of edible chemicals.

Outside, moths are arriving.
A man sleeps in his passenger seat
and I can smell the smell of the concrete, feel
the cool of the space between two days.
And a blackbird is singing about fruit
in a sycamore at the edge of the car park
over the signs indicating the direction
one must take to find the petrol,

the electricity for the electric cars
and where the road begins again,
signs I feel grateful about,
like when someone folds back a bit
on a roll of sellotape
for the next person.

Short-term lets

The air traffic controller on the beach
is not controlling air traffic.
He's blurring the tan line around
his tailbone by shifting his trunks
up and down his bum.

The colour of the sea is surprising.
Someone sells cans covered in condensation.
The waves fall like curls at the barber's.
A woman wearing a bob treads water.
The world is such a big hamster ball.

Later she washes the salt off her face
and rubs the sand from behind an ear.
The air traffic controller
holds a cup of coffee very still
over a Saturday supplement.

The sun goes down
like an Apache helicopter.
A man who to make a living
serves tzatziki to disappointed tourists
pisses against a white gate.

Behind the gate, up in the house,
a family holiday with their Doberman.
The television shows the wildfires.
The sound is piss on a gate.
The sea gets its line breaks right every time.

The mouse

Carla met me in the municipal car park.
She was wearing white Adidas shorts
and had bought a van.
We gave each other a hug.

That summer I pedalled up
hot hills in my jeans
while Carla taught aqua-aerobics
in swimming pools of grandmothers.

In the evenings we met up with Sabine
who trod on my feet mischievously.
The first night she brought us a ravishing cheese
which we had with wine and Carla's millet

and we set the mouse-trap ready for the night.

After the guests had gone we got ready for bed.
But when we put out the light, almost at once
we heard the snap. The mouse skipped, enraged
around and around in its new cage.

I took it to the corner in my pyjamas
and set it free. It bounded off
in the direction of the town centre.
The night seemed to have a lot of potential:

someone was trimming their hedge
a bit further on down the road.

Somehow I had written the times down wrong

and thirty-five minutes opened up in front of us
like a large transparent origami structure
in which we were all participating
except the girl in the one-piece outfit
handing out free slices of pie.

We walked along the road
underneath the train tracks
and the road became a car park
where a South American family were reversing in a van,
and then the car park became a forest,

the Spanish plane trees
lined up so close
they had grown tall and graceful as librarians,
the winter evening
shining in their hair.

Help

There's a man who takes all morning
walking down your road and then
he walks back again with something
round and heavy in a carrier bag.

You'd offer to help him
but you wouldn't want him to feel like he looked
as though he needed help so you don't
but he's still there, passing.

It's snowing the size and shape of cornflakes,
then it stops and the sun comes out
as if after a play to say
So, what did you think?

It's a funny time, your dad tells you,
he doesn't mean that it's April the first,
he doesn't mean that it's 2am
on the last Sunday of October.

Popping candy

It was the Wednesday on the third week
and I was looking in through the windows
at the advent calendar boxes
people had found themselves in.
One sat peering solemnly at a screen
under a parabola of bunting.
Another exercised in an upstairs window
with a set of weights, a mirror
and a side parting. And down the road,
sitting on a sofa and eating popping candy,
was a woman I knew from before all this happened.

The night set like a huge orange jelly.
In the park someone had lost a beagle.
I could hear her calling its name
again and again, but I knew
she would never find her lost dog.
The wind played with the poplars
like a pop star on a fundraiser in an African village
tenderly touching the heads of the children
and a woodpigeon flew out of them
in a great commotion, someone beginning
a round of applause at a false ending.

A couple of policemen on police horses
with little police horse riding hats
were going down the road ahead of me.
One of the horses was shitting
as it was walking. The shit just kept
bubbling up and popping out
and the policemen just kept talking.

Desert boots

By the time you can bring yourself to buy them
you need a beer so you go
to the bar you once went to
with someone you met
when you were giving blood.

Last summer it seemed
nothing would ever change
but today you are a person
who wears desert boots
and might fall in love.

You sit outside as the evening drifts in.
The pigeons bunch and slacken
in front of the precinct
and a few streetlamps blink on
like gold fillings.

Song about putting a bird in a pie

A relaxed mind is a creative mind,
says my inspiring teabag. Yours advises
to empty yourself and let the universe fill you.
We pick up the empty flowerpot on the road
and a man in a dressing gown eating tomatoes
leans out of a window and demands

that we put it back. I ask him if it's his pot.
Put it back, he shouts. *Put it back.*
Each smile is a direct achievement,
I remind him. He replies that gratitude
is the open door to abundance.
We carry on walking.

We get onto the future.
When should we panic?
Reading the tea leaves, you say that
happiness arrives when we overcome
the most impossible challenge.
Your bag has exploded.

You look at things in such a way that you are not
distracted by being looked at looking at things.
The blackbird sings a phrase then repeats it
like a monolinguist talking to a foreigner.
You can't believe anybody would even
write a song about putting a bird in a pie.

The man from the takeaway under my flat
has climbed into his bin to compress
the rubbish in order to fit more in.
He walks from one side to the other
then back again, like an animal trapped
in the hospitality industry.

Flight mode

Last thing at night she washes the writing off her hand,
pulls the pen from her hair
and lets the blinds drop
so the house can sleep.

A single brown leaf
falls out of the bonsai tree,
a haiku ending
discreetly.

She touches the lump in her lip with her tongue.
She wonders if she'll wake up with heartburn.
She imagines it glowing and pulsing inside her
as it does in the marketing materials.

Today she learned from a child
that insect populations are falling dramatically.
She's never liked insects but that isn't the same as wanting
81% to have been eliminated globally in the last 30 years.

Flight mode.
The door is shut. The gas is off.
The computers are on standby.
Her pyjamas are moons and stars;

her pyjamas are constellations and galaxies.

The laundry

It's nothing but monkey puzzle trees for miles.
We'd reach something else if we just kept walking
in one direction, but which, and in what shoes?
Nothing on the radio except at ninety one point two
an occasional sound like someone
turning the pages of a newspaper.

Each tree has a cicada, taking turns.
There is no need to wear any clothes
although sometimes we do anyway.
The swimming pool has trees growing in it.
We discover a windmill twenty miles away
which sells crisps and opens for two hours a day
exhibiting obsolete farming machinery.

We do the laundry in the sink and hang it in the barn
before the sun sets. The cicadas, proportional
in the trees, canvas emotionally.
We go indoors when the colour runs out.
The sheets dangle, still and white,
stars scratching their movements into the sky.
Drying, folding, putting away.

Acknowledgements

Many thanks to the editors of *Ambit*, *Anthropocene*, *Finished Creatures*, *Magma*, *The Moth*, *The North*, *Poetry Salzburg Review*, *The Rialto*, *Spelt*, and *Poetry Wales*, in which earlier versions of some of these poems were published. Special thanks also to Peter and Ann Sansom, Tekla Szerszynska, Daisy Hirst, Michael Laskey, John McAuliffe, Mike Mackmin, my family, and my friends.